THE BYZANTINE EMPIRE

EDITED BY
CAROLYN DECARLO

Britannica®
Educational Publishing
IN ASSOCIATION WITH
ROSEN
EDUCATIONAL SERVICES

Published in 2018 by Britannica Educational Publishing (a trademark of Encyclopædia Britannica, Inc.) in association with The Rosen Publishing Group, Inc. 29 East 21st Street, New York, NY 10010

Distributed exclusively by Rosen Publishing.
To see additional Britannica Educational Publishing titles, go to rosenpublishing.com.

First Edition

Britannica Educational Publishing
J.E. Luebering: Executive Director, Core Editorial
Andrea R. Field: Managing Editor, Compton's by Britannica

Rosen Publishing
Carolyn DeCarlo: Editor
Nelson Sá: Art Director
Brian Garvey: Designer
Cindy Reiman: Photography Manager
Nicole Baker: Photo Researcher

Library of Congress Cataloging-in-Publication Data

Names: DeCarlo, Carolyn, editor.
Title: The Byzantine Empire / edited by Carolyn DeCarlo.
Description: New York : Britannica Educational Publishing in Association with Rosen Educational Services, 2018. | Series: Empires in the Middle Ages | Includes bibliographical references and index. | Audience: Grades 5-8.
Identifiers: LCCN 2017013867| ISBN 9781680487800 (library bound : alk. paper) | ISBN 9781680488616 (pbk. : alk. paper) | ISBN 9781680488593 (6 pack : alk. paper)
Subjects: LCSH: Byzantine Empire—Civilization—Juvenile literature.
Classification: LCC DF531 .B88 2018 | DDC 949.5/02—dc23
LC record available at https://lccn.loc.gov/2017013867

Manufactured in China

Photo credits: Cover, p. 12 DEA/A. Dagli Orti/De Agositini/Getty Images; p. 5 © Hirmer Fotoarchiv, Munich; pp. 6, 40 © Encyclopaedia Britannica; p. 7 © Scala/Art Resource, New York; pp. 10, 35 DEA/G. Dagli Orti/De Agostini/Getty Images; p. 14 Universal Images Group/Getty Images; p. 15 MasterLu/Fotolia; pp. 16, 41 De Agostini Picture Library/Getty Images; p. 19 DEA/A. De Gregorio/De Agostini/Getty Images; p. 22 DEA/M. Seemuller/De Agostini/Getty Images; p. 24 © Courtesy of the trustees of the British Museum; p. 25 SuperStock/Getty Images; p. 26 Leemage/Universal Images Group/Getty Images; pp. 28–29 ullstein bild/Getty Images; p. 30 omersukrugoksu/E+/Getty Images; p. 34 Album/Oronoz/SuperStock; p. 37 Private Collection/Photo © Ken Welsh/Bridgeman Images; p. 38 Godong/Universal Images Group/Getty Images; cover and interior pages background designs Mikado767/iStock/Thinkstock (circles), Andrey_Kuzmin/Shutterstock.com (forged metal).

CONTENTS

INTRODUCTION

One of the most brilliant medieval civilizations was the Byzantine Empire. In 395 CE, the Roman Empire was divided into two parts. The Western half, ruled from Rome, fell to the tribal Germanic peoples known as barbarians in the fifth century. But the Eastern half, now known as the Byzantine Empire, lasted for more than one thousand years. In fact, the Byzantine Empire maintained its position as one of the leading civilizations in the world until its decline began in the mid-eleventh century.

In 324 CE, Constantine, the first Christian emperor, became sole ruler of the Roman Empire. He set up his Eastern headquarters in the ancient Greek colony of Byzantium in 330. The city was renamed Constantinople in his honor, and became known as the "new Rome." After the Roman Empire was formally divided sixty-five years later, Constantinople became the capital of the Byzantine Empire.

Constantinople was located on the shore of the Bosporus, midway between the Aegean and Black seas, in what is now Turkey. The city brought together people from the lands of Europe and Asia. In 1453, when the Ottoman Turks conquered the

Byzantine Empire, Constantinople became the capital of the new Ottoman Empire. The city's name was changed to Istanbul in 1930.

In their own time, the citizens of the Byzantine Empire were known as *Romaioi,* or "Romans." In their eyes, they remained firmly part of the Roman Empire despite the fact that as early as the eighth century, state and society in the East differed significantly from their earlier Roman forms. The Byzantine Romans were distinct from the Western Romans in two key ways: they spoke primarily Greek instead of Latin, and they practiced Eastern Orthodox Christianity rather than Roman Catholic Christianity. In an effort to recognize that distinction, seventeenth-century scholars renamed them and their empire "Byzantine."

A colossal marble head of Constantine the Great, 7.9 feet (2.41 meters) high, c. 313 CE. Originally, it was part of a giant statue in the Basilica of Constantine in the Roman Forum.

During the ten and a half centuries that the Byzantine Empire lasted, its boundaries continually changed. Barbarian, Western, and Arabic conquerors captured territories that were sometimes retaken by the Byzantines before being lost again. At its largest, the Byzantine Empire included Greece, Italy, Egypt, Syria, North Africa, and southern Spain. At its weakest, it consisted of just a few scattered outposts far from Constantinople. Comprising numerous ethnic groups, Byzantium was also a melting pot, and the empire was characterized during its earlier centuries by a degree of social mobility that goes against the oft-applied stereotype of a rigid, caste-based society.

The boundaries of the Byzantine Empire were constantly in flux. This map shows the extent of the empire's territory at three distinct points in its history.

Early Byzantine court dress is pictured in a mosaic that was probably completed during the sixth century. Byzantine garments were traditionally ornamented with gems and precious metals and were frequently woven with silk and gold threads.

For centuries, Byzantines enjoyed their status as the most powerful and influential people in Europe and the Middle East. Scholars preserved the literature of Rome and Greece through the darkest centuries of the Middle Ages. Statesmen developed pioneering legal codes, which were used as a basis for imperial monarchies for more than one thousand years. Artists created a distinctive style of mosaic work, painting, and domed architecture, which influenced the cultures of Greece, Italy, Spain, and Russia. The Byzantine state religion—Eastern Orthodox Christianity—became dominant in the Balkan and Russian kingdoms as well as in Greece. By the virtue of philanthropy, which the Byzantines prized and commended in their rulers, their contributions to the world were many.

CHAPTER 1

THE EARLY PERIOD: RISE OF THE BYZANTINES

The first era of the Byzantine civilization lasted from about 324 to 640 CE. During this time, the empire established its separate identity from the West. The Byzantine Empire formally split from Rome in 395, following the death of Emperor Theodosius I. His seventeen-year-old son Arcadius ruled the Eastern Empire from Constantinople, while his ten-year-old son Honorius was given the Western Empire to rule from Milan. This division, considered temporary at the time, actually remained permanent.

BARBARIC INVADERS AND RELIGIOUS DISPUTES

Conflict both at home and abroad plagued the first years of the Byzantine Empire. Hordes of barbarian people, eager for land and power, pushed at its boundaries during the fifth century. The Vandals invaded

France, Spain, and North Africa. In 455, their attack on Rome was so savage that their name has transformed into a term meaning "malicious destroyer." The Visigoths invaded Italy in 409 and later conquered France and southern Spain. The Ostrogoths also took parts of Italy, defeating the city of Ravenna in 490. A Hun attack on Constantinople itself was halted only because a plague destroyed the invading army.

These walls, built in the fifth century CE to surround and protect Constantinople, are still standing in their slightly more ruined state in a historic area of Istanbul, Turkey.

At first, the Byzantines attempted to form an uneasy peace with the barbarians who surrounded them. Theodosius II, who reigned from 408 to 450, subsidized the Huns under their chief, Attila, granting them gold in exchange for peace. It was at this time that walls were first built to surround and protect Constantinople.

While invaders threatened the foreign affairs of the Byzantines, religious arguments damaged the domestic peace of the empire. A number of heresies—ideas that are different from widely accepted beliefs—were hotly debated by churchmen and laymen alike. One of these heresies concerned the relationship of the human and divine natures of Jesus. Monophysites believed that Jesus had only one nature—one that was divine and not human. In 451 CE, a church council at Chalcedon condemned this belief as heresy.

Controversies such as that were more than religious disagreements; they were also a means of opposing the emperor, and so had political as well as religious significance. In Egypt and Syria, for example, the persistence of Monophysitism meant that Byzantine emperors faced continuing conflict with native subjects. Periodic quarrels about religious doctrine and church practice also divided Christianity between the Western (Roman Catholic) and Eastern (Eastern Orthodox) churches. These differences led to a permanent schism, or split, in 1054.

GREAT RULE: JUSTINIAN AND THEODORA

The first great period of the Byzantine Empire occurred during the reign of Justinian I, who took the throne in 527 CE and ruled until 565. Empress Theodora, his wife, was a significant presence in the empire in her own right, and ruled at his side until her death in 548. Justinian reconquered much of the territory that had fallen into barbarian hands. He also built Constantinople into a glorious city of domed churches, palaces,

This mosaic, depicting the Empress Theodora, is in the San Vitale Basilica in Ravenna, Italy. The Byzantine Empire was known for its art. Many people made pictures called mosaics out of pieces of stone.

and public arenas. By the end of his reign, the city was surrounded by a 12-mile (19-kilometer) circuit of walls. Inside, buildings of marble and alabaster grew to line spacious streets. Goods from around the world filled the shops: silk, purple cloth, and gold from Greece; spices, medicines, and precious stones from India; silks from Arabia; fur, honey, and wax from Russia; and jewelry, gold brocades, carved ivories, and rich embroideries from Constantinople itself.

The greatest of the public buildings was the Hippodrome, an arena that could seat over forty thousand people. Byzantines gathered there to sit under silk awnings and watch chariot races, jugglers, circus acts, and fights between wild animals. They also enjoyed the processions of victorious generals, who gave the crowd loot taken from vanquished enemies.

CHANGES AT HOME

A cosmopolitan city, Constantinople was home not only to Greeks and Romans, but also to Jews, Arabs, Serbs, Persians, Huns, and Scandinavians (who called the city *Miklagard*, or "Place of Enchantment"). At the same time, the rise of extreme religious orthodoxy led to persecutions of those who did not follow the strict rules of Eastern Orthodox Christianity, the state religion. Pagans throughout the empire were ordered to attend church and accept baptism, while a purge thinned their ranks in Constantinople, and masses

This nineteenth-century engraving by G.K. Richardson after W.H. Bartlett shows the Hippodrome at Constantinople in its heyday, when over forty thousand people could gather to see chariot races, fights, and processions, among other forms of entertainment.

were converted by missionaries in Asia Minor. Only Christian wives might enjoy the privileges of their dowries; Jews were denied, in addition to other civil disabilities, the privilege of testamentary inheritance unless they converted. After 391 CE, imperial decree banned the practice of non-Christian religions. By the early seventh century, the typical Byzantine city, viewed from without, actually or potentially resembled a fortress; viewed from within, it was essentially a religious community under ecclesiastical leadership.

Mosaic art was typical of Byzantine culture. Mosaics are designs made of small bits of colored stone, marble, or glass set in plaster against a background,

HAGIA SOPHIA, THE CHURCH OF THE HOLY WISDOM

The Hagia Sophia in Constantinople (now Istanbul, Turkey) was built between 532 and 537 by Anthemius of Tralles and Isodorus of Miletus for the emperor Justinian I. The minarets and wall buttresses date from the Turkish conquest in 1453.

Justinian regulated the size of churches and monasteries, forbade them to profit from the sale of property, and complained of those priests and bishops who were unlearned in the forms of the liturgy. He made great efforts to improve the quality of the secular clergy, or those who conducted the affairs of the church in the world.

In a city of churches, the most magnificent was St. Sophia Cathedral. Also known as Hagia Sophia, or the Church of the Holy Wisdom, this building still stands as an Islamic museum. It was completed by Justinian in 537 CE. It is an enormous building, shaped like a cross, with a dome reaching 180 feet (55 meters) from the ground. It has a lavish interior of colored marble, gold, silver, and beautiful mosaics.

This miniature from an Italian reproduction of Book V of the Justinian Code depicts a wedding scene. The codification of Roman laws was completed in 529 CE and is a major element in Emperor Justinian's legacy.

often of bright gold. Typical of the Byzantine style was the look of the portraits in both mosaics and paintings. Both religious and nonreligious figures were portrayed by artists as long and slim, with huge dark eyes and small mouths. Byzantine artists were also famed for their illuminated manuscripts, silver work, ivories, and sculpture.

A LASTING LEGACY

Justinian contributed more to the world than the dazzling city of Constantinople. He is perhaps best known for the Justinian Code, a collection of Roman laws from the time of the second century. This code, composed by a legal commission headed by the lawyer Tribonian, was completed in 529. The code listed all valid edicts of the time and set the legal basis for the absolute and God-given authority of an emperor over his subjects. It influenced legal theory in France, Germany, Italy, Russia, and Serbia until the nineteenth century.

Justinian hoped to recapture the lands lost to the barbarians in the fifth century, and to recreate the glory of ancient Rome. His military successes were led by a young general named Belisarius, who had begun his military career at the age of twenty-three when he defeated the Persians at the battle of Daras in 528. After that he went on to reclaim North Africa and Sicily from invaders. From 535 to 540, he retook parts of Italy, including Rome, from the Ostrogoths. In 539 he captured Ravenna, the last stronghold of the barbarians in northern Italy. He then dispatched a Gothic king, nobles, and royal treasure to Constantinople.

In 532, Justinian's reign was threatened by an uprising of hundreds of thousands of citizens during what is known as the Nika rebellion. The Nika rebellion occurred when two factions of soldiers, who were also rival horse-racing charioteers known as the Blues and the Greens, united to oppose Justinian's policies. Justinian was saved only because Empress Theodora refused to yield. At her instigation, Belisarius led troops in a massacre of thousands in the Hippodrome. Although parts of the city were destroyed in this rebellion, Justinian's victory ushered in a new era of absolute imperial rule.

During the reign of Justinian, the Byzantines recaptured parts of southern Spain and made peace with the Avars (Asian nomads) and the Persians. Many of these military gains were only temporary, however. Syria fell again to the Persians in 540, the same year that the Ostrogoths retook parts of Italy. Rome was recaptured by the Ostrogoths in 546. In 567 the Visigoths reconquered western Spain.

HERACLIUS, NEXT IN LINE

After Justinian, the next great Byzantine emperor was Heraclius, who ruled from 610 to 641. Like Justinian, he was successful in combat with enemies.

A detail from a mosaic of Justinian I and his entourage shows a group of soldiers. This mosaic dates back to the sixth century, when it was installed on a wall of the apse in the Basilica of San Vitale, Ravenna, Italy.

Heraclius faced invasions from Arabs, Avars, Bulgars, and Persians. His military organization relied on a new system first used in Asia Minor. Heraclius divided Byzantine territories into themes (army districts), which were ruled by *strategoi* (military commanders). In each theme, soldiers were given land by the government. In return, each soldier had to provide a man, a horse, and weapons for combat when called upon by the theme commander.

These themes provided the empire with an inexpensive native army and an independent class of farmers. Typically, a commander of a large theme governed ten thousand men. Themes were further divided into two brigades, each of which had five regiments. Each regiment consisted of five companies.

In 610, the year Heraclius took the throne, the prophet Muhammad began to preach to the Arabs a religion that became known as Islam. After 634, rising Islamic forces threatened the Byzantine Empire. War now became holy war between rival religions. Byzantine armies began to march behind icons—painted images of Christian holy figures—and looked to these icons for protection in battle.

CHAPTER 2

THE GOLDEN AGE: MACEDONIAN RULE

The period from about 641 to 1025 is considered to be the golden age of the Byzantine Empire. Advances in military strength, religious influence, and the arts made the empire one of the most powerful forces in the world of the Middle Ages.

The territories of the empire continued to change. Lands were lost to Islam in North Africa, Egypt, Palestine, and Syria. Arab forces besieged Constantinople in 674 and again in 717. Slavs and Bulgars threatened Byzantine holdings in the Balkans. However, Byzantine leaders were able to protect the empire. By the end of this period, the empire once again had far-flung frontiers and enormous wealth.

AGRICULTURAL ADVANCES

Despite losses, the physical changes to Byzantium's landscape were generally positive. Judging from the evidence of a document known as the Farmer's Law, dated in the seventh century, the technological base of Byzantine society was more advanced than that of contemporary western Europe: iron tools could be found in the villages; water mills dotted the landscape; and field-sown beans provided a diet rich in protein. None of those advances was to characterize western European agriculture until the tenth century. Byzantine agriculture enjoyed a highly developed tradition of careful farming that persisted even in the darkest days, enabling peasants to make the most of the soil upon which they worked.

Mosaics were not just reserved for the imperial or divine. This fifth-century mosaic depicting a farmer with hens and a basket of eggs is from the Great Palace of Constantinople—the main royal residence of the Byzantine emperors from 330 to 1081.

In fact, the invasions provided a kind of stimulus for development: having lost first its Egyptian granary and, later, its North African and Sicilian resources, the empire had to live essentially—although not totally—from whatever it could produce in the lands remaining to it. The invasions had also, in all probability, broken up many large estates, leaving small peasant holdings to become the newly normalized form of rural organization in that period. While collective village organization persisted in practice, the state seems to have made little or no attempt to bind the peasants to the soil upon which the tax registers had inscribed them. While Byzantium remained a slave-owning society, the *colonus* of the later Roman Empire had vanished, and a greater degree of freedom and mobility characterized agricultural relationships during the seventh and eighth centuries.

So it was, too, in trade and commerce. After the loss of Egypt and North Africa, the grain fleets manned by hereditary shipmasters disappeared. In their place emerged the independent merchant, of sufficient importance to call forth a code of customary law, the Rhodian Sea Law, to regulate his practices. Emperor Leo III turned back Arab assaults on the Byzantines in 718 and 740. His son and successor, Constantine V, won victories against the Arabs, Syrians, and Bulgars during his reign from 741 to 775, and in 745 Constantine reconquered Syria and, in 746, Cyprus.

BASIL I AND THE MACEDONIANS

With the coronation of Basil I of Macedonia in 867, the empire became more aware of its Greco-Roman heritage. Interest in Classical Greek scholarship had revived following the reorganization of the University of Constantinople under Emperor Michael III. After murdering Michael III, Basil secured the succession to the crown for his descendants—effectively instituting a long dynasty of Macedonian emperors. The revival was fostered and patronized particularly by the scholar-emperor Constantine VII Porphyrogenitus, who saw to the compilation of three great works on the administration, the court ceremonies, and the provinces of his empire.

This ninth-century coin features the face of Emperor Basil I.

Under the Macedonians, the Byzantine military triumphed against the Arabs to the east and the Bulgars to the north. In 880, Basil retook Italy and rebuilt the imperial army and navy. In 976, the twenty-year-old Basil II became sole ruler of the empire. His victory over the Bulgarians in 1018

THE ICONOCLASTIC CONTROVERSY

The religious identity of the Byzantines underwent profound change during this golden era. In particular, the controversy over the use of icons led to the movement called iconoclasm (image breaking). This in turn paved the way for the final split between the Roman Catholic and Eastern Orthodox churches. Iconoclasts argued that the use of icons by such leaders as Heraclius was a pagan rather than Christian ritual. Religious art, they claimed, should be only of abstract symbols, plants, or animals. They believed that the growing power of the Arabs was due to the Byzantine sin of icon worship.

A Madonna icon features the Virgin Mary decorated with beads and gemstones.

Opponents to iconoclasm, led by the monks, were called iconophiles. In 726 Emperor Leo III issued the first of many laws against the use of icons. This ushered in the Iconoclastic Controversy,

(continued on the next page)

(continued from the previous page)

which lasted until 843. In 731, the Roman pope, Gregory III, countered the uprising with a threat to expel the iconoclasts from the Catholic church.

The controversy revealed the Eastern Orthodox church to be closer in spirit to the followers of Islam, to whom the representation of God in human form was blasphemy, than to the Roman Catholic church. The Eastern church was becoming much more of a national church that saw the emperor as the union of both religious and political power. The Western church, in contrast, was independent of state authority and more international in scope.

Pope Leo III crowned Charlemagne emperor on Christmas Day, 800 CE. This painting illustrates his coronation.

It was not until 1054 that a permanent split between the two churches occurred. One indication of the future division was seen on Christmas Day in 800, when Pope Leo III crowned Charlemagne emperor of the Romans in the West. The Byzantines, who at that time were ruled by Empress Irene, ignored the claims of the new Holy Roman Empire and of the pope. It was Empress Irene who brought the Iconoclastic Controversy to an end by restoring the use of images in the Eastern Orthodox church. A further sign of dissent came in 879, when the pope of Rome and the patriarch of Constantinople expelled each other from the church by a process called excommunication.

came after a twenty-year campaign. In 1018, the Byzantines won further victories against the Lombards and Normans in Italy, and against the Bulgarians in Macedonia. The soldier-emperors of the tenth century were less interested in intellectual pursuits, but scholarship received new interest in the eleventh century.

In the time of the Macedonian emperors, Eastern Orthodox churchmen made great strides in converting pagan peoples. The conversion of the Slavs and the Bulgars to Christianity was carried out by two brothers, the Thessalonian monks Cyril and Methodius. These missionaries invented the Slavonic alphabet, an early Cyrillic alphabet also known as the Glagolitic alphabet. The new language brought literacy as well

This illustration in a manuscript depicts Saints Cyril and Methodius, two Greek brothers credited with devising the Glagolitic alphabet, the first alphabet used to transcribe Old Church Slavonic.

as Christianity to the converts. At the same time, missionary activities extended Byzantine influence to Russia and the Balkans.

AN EDUCATED CONSTANTINOPLE

Byzantine culture continued to flourish. The urban aristocracy of Constantinople, reacting against the brutalization of war, strove to make the city a center of culture and sophistication. In the arts, poetry revived and scholars produced encyclopedias, anthologies, studies of classic Greek and Roman texts, and histories. Whereas traditional pagan culture was literary and its pursuit or enjoyment thereby limited to the leisured and wealthy, the Christian liturgical celebration and its musical component were available to all, regardless of place or position. Biography, too, became both markedly Christian and markedly popular.

The University of Constantinople was endowed with a new

The University of Constantinople was founded in 425 by Theodosius II. It stood under that name until Mohammed II reestablished it as Istanbul University in 1453. The university survives to this day.

charter by Constantine IX in 1045, partly to ensure a steady flow of educated civil servants for the bureaucracy. The school of philosophy was chaired by Michael Psellus, whose research into every field of knowledge earned him a reputation for omniscience and a great following of brilliant pupils. Psellus—courtier, statesman, philosopher, and historian—is in himself an advertisement for the liveliness of Byzantine society in the eleventh century.

Mosaics and paintings were influenced by a new church decoration style, in which the church itself represented the world and the dome represented heaven.

In this scheme, a portrait of Christ as Lord of All (Pantocrator) stared down at worshipers from the dome; the church walls were covered with portraits of other holy figures.

The Macedonians developed a revision of the Justinian Code, known as the Basilica, and abolished the last vestige of the old Roman Republic—the Senate. A centralized and highly ritualized bureaucracy helped the emperor to control an elaborate foreign and diplomatic service. There were by now more than thirty army districts in Europe and Asia directly responsible to the emperor in Constantinople. By the opening decades of the second millennium, the Byzantines had reached the peak of their power.

CHAPTER 3

DECLINE AND FALL

The era from about 1025 to 1453 witnessed the decline of the Byzantine Empire and its ultimate destruction. Loss of territory, internal discord, and defeats by the crusaders were blows from which the empire could not recover. There were new enemies in this era—the Petcheneg and Seljuk Turks to the east and north, and the Normans and Slavs to the west. In 1064 the Byzantines lost Belgrade to the Hungarians. In 1071 a Turkish victory at the battle of Manzikert ended Byzantine control in Asia Minor. Also in 1071, the Byzantines lost their last territory in Italy to Norman invaders.

ETHNIC AND RELIGIOUS HOSTILITY

Internal politics of the empire contributed to its growing weakness. After the death of Basil II in 1025, fifteen emperors reigned in the fifty-six years until 1081. The rise of Alexius I Comnenus to power in 1081 restored some stability to Constantinople. The Comnenus family ruled for the next century, until 1185.

In 1054, the final schism between the churches of Rome and Constantinople occurred. Led by Pope Leo IX and Cardinal Humbert, the papal legate to Constantinople, the Roman church excommunicated the head of the Eastern Orthodox church, Patriarch Michael Cerularius. By this time, the churches differed on a number of important doctrines, including the celibacy of clergy.

Bitter ethnic and religious hostility marked the history of the empire's later centuries. The Crusades, inspired by the Roman Catholic church, undermined the power of the Byzantine Empire even further. In 1096 the First Crusade, consisting of some thirty thousand persons, converged on Constantinople before going to the Holy Land to free it of Arab domination. Emperor Alexius I Comnenus provided supplies for the crusaders, but he failed to obtain a promise from them to recover any of the empire's former territories that they might conquer. The crusaders, partially out of hostility toward the Eastern Orthodox church, proceeded to raid Byzantine lands on their way to Palestine.

Tensions between the Byzantine Empire and the Holy Roman Empire were further fueled when disagreements about trading rights in the Mediterranean Sea led to a war with Venice in 1171. By the Fourth Crusade from 1202 to 1204, these hostilities

This illustration depicts Michael Cerularius' ascension to the position of patriarch in 1043, surrounded by clergymen. The head of the Eastern Orthodox church would later be excommunicated from the Roman church in 1054, a final schism between the churches culminating from a number of doctrinal differences.

had reached such a point that the crusaders invaded and conquered Constantinople. After much looting and destruction, the crusaders established a Latin Empire in the city under the rule of Count Baldwin of Flanders. This so-called empire was confined to the city of Constantinople; loyal citizens of the Byzantine Empire relocated in Asia Minor and Greece and in the kingdom of Trebizond near the Black Sea.

In exile, the empire at Nicaea became a manageable and almost self-sufficient unit, with a thriving economy based on agriculture and, latterly, on trade with the Seljuqs. It had no navy but the land frontiers in Anatolia, policed by well-paid troops, were stronger than they had been since the twelfth century.

A RETURN TO CONSTANTINOPLE

However, to leave Constantinople in foreign hands long-term was unthinkable. In 1261, a force under

The ruins of the walls and North Gate of the ancient city of Nicaea, in present-day Iznik, Turkey, are shown here.

Emperor Michael VIII Palaeologus reconquered Constantinople and destroyed the Latin Empire of the crusaders. A new dynasty was founded, and Michael was determined that it should succeed. After the dismemberment of the empire by the Fourth Crusade, the city was no longer the focal point of an integrated structure. It was more like an immense city-state in the midst of a number of more or less independent provinces. Therefore, Michael took measures for the rehabilitation, repopulation, and defense of Constantinople. He stimulated a revival of trade by granting privileges to Italian merchants.

There followed a final flowering of Byzantine culture. The Eastern church was now secure in its independence from the Roman Catholic church. The patriarchs of Constantinople were respected by other Orthodox churchmen throughout the East. There was a renewed interest in classical Greek learning and a revival of the arts, especially mosaics and painting.

WARS IN THE HOMELAND

From 1341 to 1347, civil war destroyed what was left of the Byzantine economy and domestic peace. In 1341 the nine-year-old son of Andronicus III Palaeologus became emperor as John V Palaeologus. He was challenged by his guardian, John VI Cantacuzenus, who rallied a group of religious fanatics called Zealots (mystic Christians, also called Hesychasts) to side

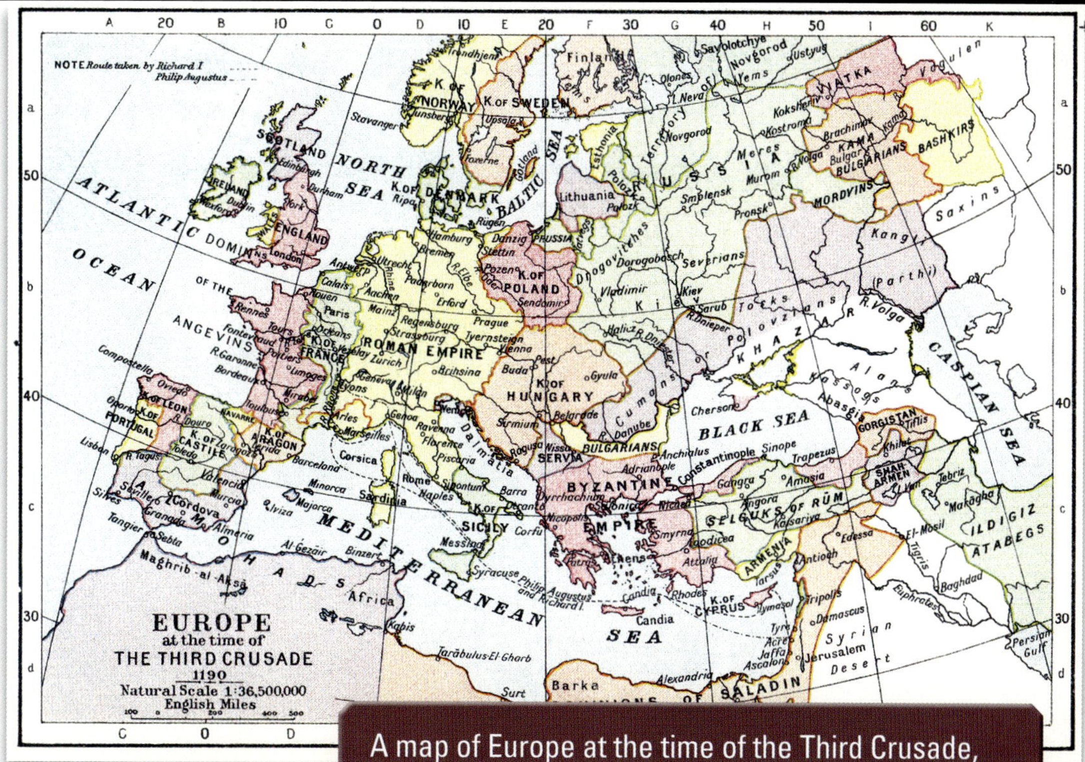

A map of Europe at the time of the Third Crusade, 1190 CE, shows the boundaries of the Byzantine Empire as they were then.

with him in his quest for the throne. The Orthodox clergymen sided with John V and his mother, Anna of Savoy. The resulting civil war led to Cantacuzenus' victory, but at great cost. The empire was ravaged by war and dissent, and new attacks by the Serbs, Turks, and Genoese threatened remaining territories. At the same time, in 1347, the great epidemic known as the Black Death decimated the population of Constantinople and other parts of the empire. Cantacuzenus, nevertheless, did what he could to restore

A CULTURAL REVIVAL: MYSTICISM

Materially, the empire seemed almost beyond hope of recovery in the early fourteenth century, but spiritually and culturally it showed a remarkable vitality. The church, no longer troubled over the question of union with Rome, grew in prestige and authority.

There was a new flowering of the Byzantine mystical tradition in a movement known as Hesychasm, whose chief spokesman was Gregory Palamas, a monk from Athos. The theology of the Hesychasts (also known as Zealots) was thought to be heterodox

An Eastern Orthodox icon depicts St. Gregory Palamas' death.

by some theologians, and a controversy arose in the first half of the fourteenth century that was as disruptive to the church and state as the earlier Iconoclastic dispute had been.

The revival of mystical speculation and the monastic life may have been in part a reaction against the contemporary revival of secular literature and learning. Scholarship of all kinds was patronized by Andronicus II. As in the eleventh century, interest was mainly centered on a rediscovery of ancient Greek learning.

A notable exception was Demetrius Cydones who—like Michael Psellus—managed affairs of state for a number of emperors for close to fifty years. Cydones translated the works of Thomas Aquinas into Greek; he was the forerunner of a minority of Byzantine intellectuals who joined the Roman Church and looked to the West to save their empire from ruin.

the stability of the empire. But by 1400 only Constantinople, Salonika, and parts of southern Greece remained in the empire.

The end of the Byzantine Empire came on May 29, 1453. On that day, the Ottoman Turks, led by the Sultan Mohammed II, invaded Constantinople. Walls that had held firm in the early Middle Ages against German, Hun, Avar, Slav, and Arab invaders were breached finally by modern artillery. By transporting their boats over land to join Ottoman assault forces, the Turks bypassed an iron chain stretched across

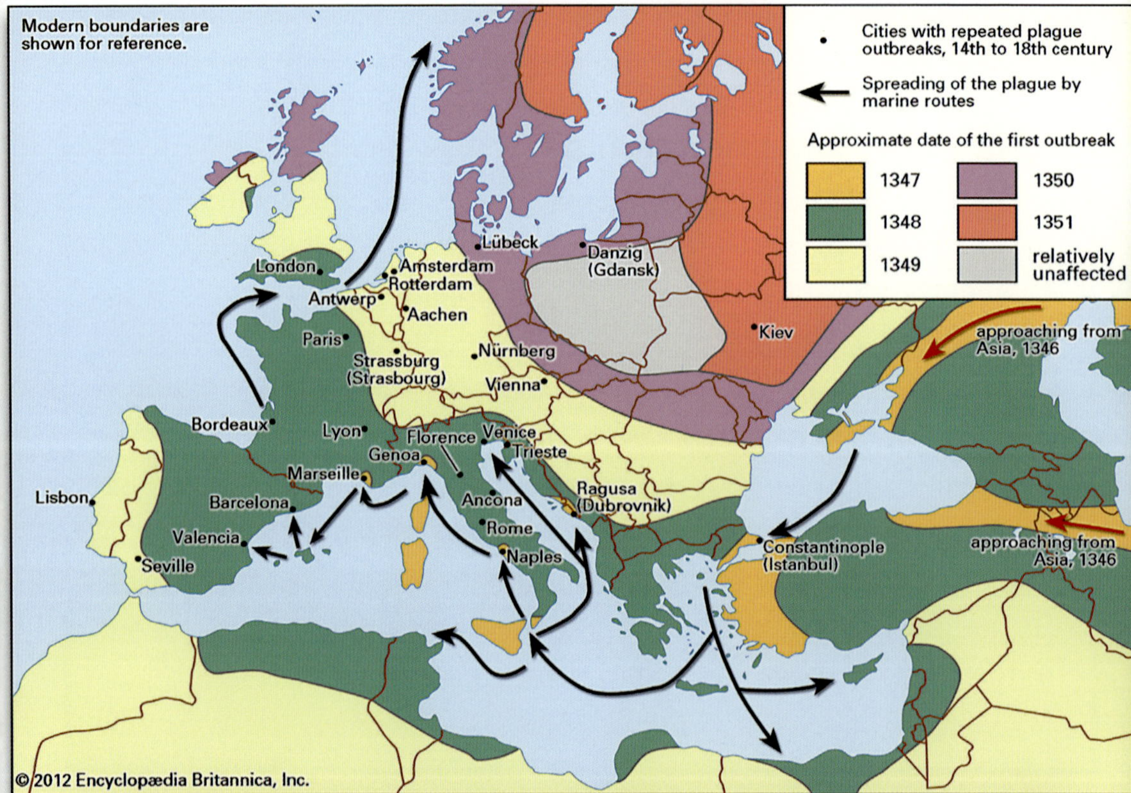

The reach of the Black Death in Europe from 1347 to 1351 can be seen as it spread year by year. Constantinople received its first outbreak in 1347 via mariners approaching from Asia over the Black Sea.

the waters leading to the city. They used a cannon that was 26 feet (8 meters) long to fire 1,200-pound (545-kilogram) cannonballs at the walls of Constantinople. The last emperor, Constantine XI Palaeologus, was killed fighting in the city's defense.

The Turks plundered the city for three days. Then they replaced the cross—symbol of the Christians—

This miniature depicts Sultan Mohammed II's troops laying siege to Constantinople in 1453 CE.

with the crescent—symbol of Islam—over St. Sophia. A few Byzantine outposts fell to the Turks shortly after: Athens in 1456; Morea in 1460; and Trebizond in 1461. With these communities gone, the last remnants of the Byzantine Empire finally collapsed. However, its contributions to religion, art and architecture, and political thought endured as a legacy to the world.

barbarian Of or relating to a land, culture, or people alien and usually believed to be inferior to another land, culture, or people; lacking refinement, learning, or artistic or literary culture.

colonus A tenant farmer in the later Roman Empire who was bound to the land and obliged to pay a rent usually in produce.

dowry The money, goods, or estate that a woman brings to her husband in marriage.

ecclesiastical Of or relating to a church, especially as an established institution.

excommunication An ecclesiastical judgment depriving a person of the rights of church membership.

Hellenize To make Greek or Hellenistic in form or culture.

heresy Adherence to a religious opinion contrary to church doctrine.

heterodox Contrary to or different from an acknowledged standard, a traditional form, or an established religion.

iconoclasm The doctrine, practice, or attitude of a person who destroys religious images or opposes their veneration.

iconophile A person who supports or is in favor of religious images or icons and their veneration; in opposition to an iconoclast.

legate An official representative (as an ambassador or envoy).

monastic Of or relating to monasteries, or to monks or nuns.

mysticism The belief that direct knowledge of God or of spiritual truth can be achieved through meditation, intuition, or some other state that takes an individual beyond a normal consciousness.

patronize To act as patron of; to provide aid or support for.

secular Of or relating to worldly or temporal concerns; not overtly or specifically religious.

strategos A Greek army leader or military general.

Vandal A member of a Germanic people who lived in the area south of the Baltic Sea between the Vistula and the Oder rivers; overran Gaul, Spain, and northern Africa in the fourth and fifth centuries CE.

Zealot A member of a fanatical sect arising in Judea during the first century CE and militantly opposing the Roman domination of Palestine.

FOR FURTHER READING

Belezos, Dimitris. *Byzantine Armies 325 AD–1453 AD* (Military Essays). Carrollton, TX: Squadron/Signal Publications, 2009.

Connor, Carolyn L. *Women of Byzantium*. New Haven, CT: Yale University Press, 2004.

Garland, Lynda. *Byzantine Empresses: Women and Power in Byzantium AD 527-1204* (Reprint Edition). London, UK: Routledge, 2011.

Gregory, Timothy E. *A History of Byzantium* (Second Edition). Hoboken, NJ: Wiley-Blackwell, 2010.

Kovacs, Vic. *The Culture of the Byzantine Empire* (Ancient Cultures and Civilizations). New York, NY: Rosen Publishing, 2017.

Oman, Charles. *The Byzantine Empire*. CreateSpace Independent Publishing Platform, 2016.

Romane, Julian. *Byzantium Triumphant: The Military History of the Byzantines 959-1025*. Barnsley, UK: Pen and Sword, 2015.

Samuels, Charlie. *Timeline of the Middle Ages*. New York, NY: Gareth Stevens, 2010.

VanVoorst, Jenny Fretland. *The Byzantine Empire*. North Mankato, MN: Compass Point Books, 2013.

Vescia, Monica. *The Rise and Fall of the Byzantine Empire* (The Rise and Fall of Empires). New York, NY: Rosen Publishing, 2016.

WEBSITES

Because of the changing nature of internet links, Rosen Publishing has developed an online list of websites related to the subject of this book. This site is updated regularly. Please use this link to access this list:

http://www.rosenlinks.com/EIMA/Byzantine

INDEX